ETHEREAL MUSINGS

MALAVIKA JAYASREE

Contents

Contents

ETHEREAL MUSINGS

Foreword

O. S. Unnikrishnan

Chairman of the Kerala Folklore Academy

Poetry often becomes the voice of the soul, a bridge between thought and emotion, a gentle echo of one's innermost reflections, dreams, and memories in the stillness between chaos and clarity. Malavika Jayasree's poetry collection is a luminous journey across that bridge. With each verse, she draws us into a world of introspection, healing, love, and quiet strength. These twenty poems are more than a mere collection of words; they are vivid, breathing moments immortalized in ink. From the fierce rebirth in *The Wildflower* to the surreal escape of *Stargazing*, Malavika Jayasree gracefully explores the intricacies of the human spirit. Her words reflect a soul that has wandered through shadows, sought light in the labyrinth of the heart, and returned bearing the gift of insight.

The spirit of resilience that infuses much of this collection is introduced in the opening poem, *The Wildflower*. Here, the image of a wildflower enduring the summer heat and emerging like a phoenix sets the tone for the journey ahead, a poetic voice that remains unshaken in the face of adversity. It is both a portrait of survival and a reminder that beauty can bloom even in hardship. Themes of nature, duality, nostalgia, and inner fire recur throughout, binding each poem with emotional honesty. This collection offers not only poetic expression but also companionship for the reader's inner journey. In *Inner Ignition*, for example, she delves into the soul's yearning, where dreams fuel a fire that lights the darkest nights. It speaks of determination, a steady, internal flame, not merely of hope.

A meta-poetic moment arrives in *The Return to Ink*, where the act of writing becomes a return to the self rather than just a pastime, as the poet reclaims her voice after a pause. Similarly, *A Glint of Hope* expresses the quiet strength found in everyday life. Beneath the ordinary rhythm, a flicker persists, propelling the soul onward. In *Missing Memories*, the poet evokes festive nostalgia, illustrating how joy, though momentarily absent, leaves behind a comforting echo. This thread of hope weaves through again. *A Pilgrimage* takes us on a sacred, introspective journey where turning inward becomes an act of spiritual reverence, and dreams are venerated. With *The Boon*, our focus shifts outward. Nature, particularly the sky, is portrayed as a source of healing and limitless possibility. This idea deepens in *Seeds of Soul*, where dreams are envisioned as firmly rooted and alive, nurtured by blood, soul, and longing. In *A Love Tale*, love becomes a dreamlike realm, elusive, painful, and yet eternally cherished. Its tone is haunting, marked by a wistfulness that lingers.

She is an ode to the emotional complexity of the feminine self. Here, the poet paints herself or a muse in rich hues: sentimental, whimsical, luminous, and unshakably strong. Womanhood is not confined but celebrated in all its raw truth. In *The Magical World*, the poet imagines an emotional refuge where healing is melodic and love is never lost. This world is not escapist, but cathartic, shaped by the rhythm of a dreaming heart. *Whispers of Heart* follows as a profound exploration of inner conflict, emotional entanglement, and the hope for peace and emotional release rendered with eloquence.

With warmth and wisdom, Malavika Jayasree reminds us that even in life's fragmented moments, beauty can be found and strength reclaimed. These are poems to revisit, to reflect with, and to be moved by again and again. Each one offers a window into the poet's inner world, capturing moments of wonder, joy, longing, and deep introspection. This collection carries a cadence that mirrors the human experience, inviting us to pause, feel, and see both the world and ourselves more clearly. To write poetry is to bare one's soul to the world to find beauty in vulnerability, strength in silence, and meaning in the spaces between words. As a new poet steps into this timeless craft, they do more than share verses; they open a door to their inner world and invite us in. I hope that this work serves not only as a source of inspiration but also as a reliable pathfinder for new writers of the English language.

Author

Malavika Jayasree

Malavika Jayasree is a promising voice in contemporary literature from the state of Kerala, India. She holds a master's degree in Botany from Mahatma Gandhi University, where she was a rank holder during her postgraduate studies. Currently, she is pursuing a Ph.D. in Medico-Botany at Bharathiar University in Coimbatore, Tamil Nadu. A multifaceted talent, Malavika was also awarded the title of Kalathilakam at the Sahodaya Kalotsavam, recognising her excellence in the arts. This unique blend of science and creativity informs her writing, allowing her to weave intricate connections between the natural world and the human experience.

From an early age, Malavika displayed a profound passion for literature, winning numerous accolades in poetry competitions at both school and college levels. Her talent was particularly recognised when she received the state-level prize for the best poem from the Kerala Coconut Development Board, Government of Kerala, a significant achievement that marked the beginning of her literary journey. She also showed her signature in classical music and classical dance, especially in Bharatanatyam. Her poetry, characterised by vivid imagery and emotional depth, has found its way into various literary magazines, both in Malayalam and English. She has also contributed to two international anthologies: *Delusion* and *Music the Elixir of Life*, where her poems captivated readers with their enchanting themes and lyrical quality.

Malavika's work resonates with those who appreciate the beauty of nature and the intricate dance of life. As she continues to develop her unique voice, her contributions to literature promise to inspire and connect with readers around the globe. With a harmonious blend of scientific insight and poetic flair, Malavika Jayasree is undoubtedly a literary figure to watch in the coming years. Her husband Dr. Saran S., is a writer, Poet, Nature Activist and Assistant Professor in English at the University of Kerala.

Malavika Jayasree

Dedication

To my dearest mother, **Jayasree Pallikkal**, whose unwavering love and boundless wisdom have been the nurturing soil for my dreams. Your strength and grace have inspired every verse and breathed life into my words. My mother was the silent strength behind every step I have taken, the gentle force behind every word I have written. Your love, resilience, and unwavering belief in me are the roots of all I am and all I hope to become

To my beloved father, **P. P. Rajendran Nair**, whose guidance and quiet encouragement have been the compass that steered me through every storm. Your steadfast belief in me has been a beacon of hope and inspiration.

To my cherished husband, **Dr. Saran S.**, whose love and support have been the steadfast rhythm behind every line. Your unwavering faith and gentle understanding have been my greatest muse and my truest companion.

With all my love and gratitude,

Malavika Jayasree

Contents

Prologue

In the quiet areas between moments, in which the pulse of existence slows to a gentle murmur, there exists a realm of phrases and whispers. This collection of poems emerges from that very realm, a tapestry woven from threads of emotion, mirrored images, and desires. Here, each poem is a fraction of a larger journey, an exploration of the human spirit's boundless ability to feel, to yearn, and to transcend.

These poems are like wildflowers, resilient and vibrant, flourishing amidst the shadows of doubt and the brilliance of hope. They echo the struggles and triumphs of the soul, the quiet battles fought within the labyrinth of the thoughts, and the serene revelations located in moments of stillness. Each piece captures a unique aspect of our shared revel, from the fiery determination of a phoenix growing through its ashes to the mild introspection of stargazing dreams.

As you switch those pages, you'll locate yourself navigating through the essence of life, from the delicate dance of internal desires to the grand pilgrimage of self-discovery. The verses right here are not mere phrases, however, they are alive with the breath of human experience breath that is both fleeting and eternal.

Allow yourself to be carried through the seasons of emotion and thought, to wander through the enchanted forests of reminiscence and wish. Embrace the sparkle of ideas that shines through the cracks of life's challenges and the serene balm of moments well-lived.

In this prologue, let those poems be your manual, your solace, and your spark. Here, within the dance of ink and notion, you can also locate reflections of your journey and solace in your very own heart.

Welcome to this poetic voyage, it resonates deeply and inspires you because it has stimulated me.

Acknowledgements

With deepest gratitude, I first thank **God,** whose infinite grace and guidance made this journey possible.

My heartfelt thanks to **Shri O. S. Unnikrishnan**, Chairman of the Kerala State Folklore Academy, for his gracious foreword and inspiring words, which have enriched the essence of this book.

To my beloved **Parents and In-laws**, your love, sacrifices, and unwavering support have been the foundation of my life and this creative endeavour.

I am deeply grateful to my guide, **Dr. K. Thenmozhi,** for her constant encouragement and for providing the space and time to cultivate our talents and extracurricular pursuits alongside academic research.

A special note of appreciation to my husband, **Dr. Saran S.**, not only for being my unwavering support but also for his meticulous work as the editor of this book. Your keen eye, thoughtful suggestions, and dedication to refining every word have elevated this collection to its fullest expression. Thank you for walking beside me in both life and literature.

Finally, to my dear **friends**, thank you for your encouragement, warmth, and presence. Your support has illuminated this journey.

This book is a reflection of all your blessings, and I carry each of you in every word written.

1. Inner Ignition

Amidst my deepest thoughts, I roamed,
Into the realm where shadows danced and the light was sown,
Where whispers of my heart were gently known,
And secrets of my soul were quietly shown.
I traveled miles beyond the distant shore,
Through the labyrinth of my inner core,
With desires that burned and longed for more,
Seeking to mend what was once sore.
Engraved in the hardest stone,
In corners where my fears had grown,
New dreams and hopes were softly sown,
By the heart's light, they were brightly shown.
These dreams ignited a flame within,
A fire that burned with a fervent grin,
Illuminating paths I'd yet to begin,
And lighting the dark where doubts had been.
To travel an extra mile, so steep,
In reality's rugged terrain so deep,
Where doubts and fears would creep,
And the journey felt like a troubled sleep.
Yet still I walked through the darkest night,
With dreams as my beacon, burning bright,

Guiding me through every challenging fight,
Leading me to my inner light.
Through fire and rain, I emerged anew,
Stronger, with a heart that grew,
Fueled by dreams that my soul knew,
And gave me the strength to see them through.

2. The wildflower

She was a wildflower,
An enchanting one with.
Alluring and amazing beauty;
She was loved by everyone, but.
During the dry summer times,
Her petals lost their color.
And was surrounded by crinkles.
But she wasn't bewildered!
She started fighting endlessly,
Deciding to fly like
A phoenix through the
Ashes of her deep burns.
Carrying even the subtle memories,
That rejuvenates her soul.
Leaving all crashes and scratches,
As a reminder forever.
After ages and ages, as a reminiscence
Of triumph and happiness.

3. The Return to Ink

Ever since I left my pen for a while,
My soul eloped to an alternative world.
The one full of intuitions and
Unresolved thoughts.
There are several questions,
Raised in front of me, I saw my alter-ego,
Conquering the never-ending war of thoughts,
As it wrestled with the silent echoes of doubt.
The errands of the mind might be unclear,
But after a long time, in a twist of fate,
My soul returned to where it was meant to be,
To the tip of my pen, where peace awaits.

4. Breath of Bliss

Stay on my lap
Until the next dawn,
Search for my soul
Through the warmth of my breath.
Sit closer and hug tight,
Leave all melancholy behind,
Bloom from within like
An alluring marigold in spring.
Hold together and grow together,
Be more serene and share the bliss,
In the gentle embrace of the morning light,
Where hearts entwine and sorrows dismiss.

5. Alter-ego

Hey alter-ego, why did we meet in
The middle of the chaos?
Why were you reluctant to?
Take that mask off for just a few seconds.
To me, you were someone I
Had known for years,
Perhaps we share the same
Origin and a common fragile heart.
Carrying pure red-hot blood,
Hiding is just a temporary guise,
Emerging is uniqueness,
Dealing is strength, and chaos is real.
Next time, take off that mask,
Dear alter-ego, we have no differences.
Let's move on and conquer together,
United in purpose, strong and free.

6. A Glint of Hope

Wander and wonder for the time being!
Just you and your shadow,
Entangled in the single loop of life,
Passing days of tranquility, trying to be serene.
In this bustling world of happenings,
Some days are indolent, some splendid,
And others leave you worn out,
Yet still, a glint remains to move on.
Through the ebb and flow of each day,
In the quiet moments and the chaos,
Keep that spark alive within,
Every twilight brings a new dawn.

7. Missing Memories

What are you seriously missing?
Is it that sudden trembling rise?
In your heartbeat when you saw
The shining bells on the Christmas tree,
Ages ago as a small kid?
Or is it an unfinished dream,
Of a mistletoe kiss from a blurry-faced guy.
In your teenage fantasies,
Lost to time's gentle passing?
Or perhaps it's those blissful Christmas eves,
Celebrated with your young, crazy friends
In your hostel yard, under the frosty sky?
It's cold outside, but still, you feel the warmth inside.
The constant warmth from a bundle of memories,
Offers a reminiscence of cool friendship.
Bliss, forgiveness, and the elation of Thanksgiving,
Now only exists as missing memories.

8. Essence of Being

Let her mind find its autumn,
Let it soar up to infinity,
Embracing the pure essence of
Those midnight scribblings.
Carrying the thick and thin moments of life,
Let it admire the uniqueness within,
Watching the shine from deep inside,
Unrestricted, let it fly.
Without boundaries, let it ascend,
Until it meets its final destiny,
Tracing the path of its own making,
Finding peace in its boundless journey.

9. The Eternal Horizon

Walking amid darkness,
Searching the horizon of extreme cheerfulness,
Moving forward-alone, fearless, contented,
Gazing at the alluring constellations that
Pave the pathway with their enormous shine.
Along the way, I found a broken piece of mirror,
Reflecting in the silver starlight,
Took a piece and looked at it.
In that moment, I discovered the real horizon,
The horizon of eternal happiness,
Revealed in my reflection,
A beacon of joy amidst the night's expanse.

10. A Pilgrimage

I nurtured my dreams for a long,
With glimmering memories,
Tons of enthusiasm and emotions,
True reflections of life.
Entangled with love, sorrows, and joys,
Yet the sorrows were persistent and remained.
Now I'm nurturing my dreams again,
Embarking on a long and sacred journey.
Keeping my dreams with respect,
I dive into my tranquil depths,
Reflecting the real inside me-
Yes, it's a pilgrimage to my depth.

11. The Boon

When the rhythm of our hearts rises,
Just raise our heads, take a deep breath,
And look up there is a boon!
Given by the holy hands; nothing but,
The vast and serene silent sky,
With blue depths and white feathers.
We can either swim into its deep blues,
Or fly on those white feathery clouds.
It's our choice; two beautiful choices!
Simply an escape from all agony,
Take a trip to the alluring sky,
To break all crux life's ways.

12. Embers of Love

Though the world around me may chill,
Your warmth is my heart's thrill.
Frozen wings, I sought solace in your flame,
Waiting at a pearl-encrusted shore, where love's name was claimed.
They called me 'Desire,' a title I adored,
But when duty called, I'll depart, with a tender kiss implored.
I'll hold a piece of you, a treasured heart's share,
Merging our souls—without you, I'd be lost, with no one to care!

13. Seasons

Each season is an experience,
Leaving behind a trail of memories.
Many have passed, with nothing to hold,
Unspoken, like the departed spring breeze.
The withered leaves, the fallen flowers,
The summer that merged and faded,
None of these are lost, for I have
Stored them within my soul.
Later, they will reflect on me,
I will become a season,
Transforming, evolving, like time,
A mirror to the cycles that I have lived.

14. Seeds of Soul

Sow the seeds of dreams, not in bare land,
But in the deepest corner of the heart,
Where blood stains smell and soul whispers.
Let them grow and bloom into a dream-creeper.
With crimson red petals and the fragrance of desires,
They never wilt or wither,
Their petals deeply blending
Into the depths of the soul constantly.
That's why they were named as seeds of the soul,
Everlasting and vibrant,
Rooted in the essence of who we are,
Nurturing dreams that endure through time.

15. A Love Tale

In the depths of my heart, where shadows reside,
A dream appeared, and I saw your face.
Like a wonder, it unfolded beyond words,
Your memories, a treasure trove, I hold tight.
In the darkness, a light flickered, a sprout grew,
A gentle breeze whispered secrets of our love.
Like a mirage, it vanished, leaving me with pain,
Yet, I still search for that fleeting dream again.
Oh, the vast expanse of the sky, so mysterious and wide,
This small world, a mere droplet in the ocean's tide.
I'm lost in the whirlpool of my mind,
Yet, I still yearn for that love so hard to find.
In the silence, I hear your voice, a gentle breeze,
A whispered promise of love's sweet release.
My heart flutters like a bird set free,
In your love, my soul finds solace, wild and carefree.

16. She

Her thoughts are often sentimental,
A world of emotions where love resides,
Nostalgia's warmth, a gentle breeze,
Shaping her heart, where memories abide.
Some of them induce the elation of the soul,
A symphony of joy where spirits unfold,
The feeling of perfect ecstasy,
A state of bliss where love is told.
That rebuilds her mind and body,
Restoring vitality like a work of art,
Rejuvenating her essence with a radiant glow,
Illuminating her path, a gentle start.
But some create misty eyes,
Afloat in tears and melancholy,
A sea of emotions where waves crash and roar,
A heart that's heavy with secrets untold once more.
This might change her into a weirdo,
A soul quirky with emotions untamed,
A heart unconventional with love unashamed,
A spirit free with a beauty unclaimed.
But her glory remains forever,
A light that shines bright like a beacon in flight,

Guiding her way through life's plodding night,
Illuminating her essence, a radiant delight.

17. The Magical World

In the twilight's hush, where shadows play,
When the rhythm of our hearts rises,
A gentle whisper paves a secret way,
To the magical world of beats and melodies.
In this sweet realm,
The heart finds its home,
Where all emotion merges together,
And love is never unknown.
A world where the soul takes flight,
And thoughts dive deep into fictional reality,
Of soft caresses that heal the heart's deep pain,
And summon memories like summer rain.
In that gentle embrace,
Our hearts will thrive and heal,
Cherishing a profound mirth and pleasure,
Away from all worries and pressure.

18. Whispers of Heart

Why don't you just divert the path,
From the mystic corners of my heart,
Where shadows dance and secrets start,
And the whispers of my soul never depart.
Stuffed with subtle emotions,
Like a canvas, rich and deep,
A kaleidoscope of feelings in motion,
Ebbing and flowing like the ocean's sweep.
Overflowing illusions,
Like a dream that's hard to define,
Ephemeral moments lost in time,
Leaving me with memories so divine.
And drama,
Like a play where actors roam,
A stage of life where stories unfold,
And the plot thickens as the heart grows old.
Can you just lead me away,
From this maze of emotions, I've made,
To a place of calm where love is displayed,
And the heart can heal in a peaceful shade.
Through the labyrinth of my mind,
Where thoughts and feelings intertwine,

Guide me gently with a loving hand,
To a refuge where I can stand.

19. Stargazing

Every day, she yearns to wake,
In a fantasy world, her heart's at stake,
A realm of happiness, serene and bright,
Free from chaos, where love shines like a light.
She dreams of opening her eyes to a sunny day,
Where joy never grows old, and worries drift away,
A stroll through gardens, paved and fair,
Where butterflies smile and bees dance in the air.
A world of ecstasy, pure and true,
Where dreams unfold and magic shines through,
But alas, she knows not all dreams come real,
So she creates her own, her heart's reveal.
By stargazing, she builds her fantasy world,
A realm of wonder where love unfurls,
A place to escape where dreams take flight,
In the night sky's twinkling, celestial light.

20. Arboreal Realm

She welcomed me warmly,
Welcomed me artistically,
Though I loved her very much,
She never attempted to hesitate.
I ogled at her all day,
And sat up all night,
To write about her beauty,
She never found my love.
One year passed-winter,
Summer, and autumn,
Before the appearance of spring,
I met her again at dawn.
She looked cool and tranquil,
Her eye-tail perplexed my soul.
I stared at her tailed eyes,
Her face haunts me again and again.
I tried to depend on evil,
To forget her image,
But an appetite for her
Keeps me from finding peace.
An evil with a charming face and smile,
With tall hair defying gravitation,

I noticed her teeth coming out,
Dizzy raptures overwhelmed me.
I requested her recompense,
But she looked at me with a wild face,
There was a laugh behind the wild,
And it never scared me.
Even though I am a rebel,
I never revealed my folly in her presence.
May my captious mind be destroyed by her beauty,
I can hear it all day.
Again, she gave me the same opportunity,
To meet her and share my feelings.
I found different characters in you,
But your children cared for me well.
I thank your children for their care,
For the protection they showed in the copse.
But I lack the presence of a few,
In the wretches of smoke and woods.
You showed me her again,
My eyes haunt her on the way.
She diverged with a smile,
I re-touched my old memories.